T0147189

MY CUSTOMER SPEECH

SPEECH

A LEGACY OF GLASS

BERNIE KEATING

authorHOUSE®

AuthorHouse™
1663 Liberty Drive
Bloomington, IN 47403
www.authorhouse.com
Phone: 1 (800) 839-8640

Published by AuthorHouse 04/19/2019

ISBN: 978-1-7283-0911-8 (sc)
ISBN: 978-1-7283-0912-5 (hc)
ISBN: 978-1-7283-0910-1 (e)

ALSO BY BERNIE KEATING:

Strike Vote. Unpublished 1962

The Holy Grail was a Paper Cup. Unpublished 1971

When America Does It Right. AIIE Press, Atlanta, GA, 1978

Riding the Fence Lines. BWD Publishing LLC, Toledo, OH, 2003

Buffalo Gap Frontier: Crazy Horse to NoWater to the Roundup. Pine Hills Press, Sioux Falls, SD, 2008

1960's Decade of Dissent: The Way We Were.
     AuthorHouse Publishing (AH P), Bloomington, IN, 2009

Songs and Recipes: For Macho Men Only. AH P, 2010

Rational Market Economics. AH P, 2011

Music: Then and Now. AH P, 2011

A Romp Thru Science: Plato and Einstein to Steve Jobs.
     AH P, 2012

Riding My Horse: Growing up in Buffalo Gap. AH P, 2013

Searching for God. AH P, 2013

Chasing Tumbleweeds. AH P, 2014

Ebenezer Sackett's Christmas Carol. AH P, 2015

They Rode with Custer. AH P, 2016

Echoes. AH P, 2016

Pivot to Asia. Author House Publishing, 2017

My Autoimmune Stuff. Author House Publishing, 2017

Milestones. Author House Publishing, 2018

Dissertation on Writing. Author House Publishing, 2018

My Take on the Past, Author House Publishing, 2019

FOREWORD

I was looking through old files recently and the only speech I kept from my 50 years of working for O-I (Owens-Illinois) was the 1984 speech delivered to the Coca Cola executive management group in Atlanta Georgia. I don't recall why I kept that particular speech, but much of the technical and historical stuff is still pertinent. Unfortunately, the slide contents were lost and you must use your visual imagination.

My thoughts while on the podium are little changed, caught in a time capsule of 35 years.

Recently turning ninety years of age, I'm one of the few still active from that era of the 1950's when we set the stage for the technical developments that were to lead to the O-I industry dominance. Milestones have a way of becoming lost to future generations. To prevent that was a motivation for recording the legacy of that evolving time in the history of glass.

Bernie Keating

1984: COCA COLA ATLANTA GEORGIA

I walked to the podium following the introduction and began my speech.

> [*"It is a pleasure to be with you to talk on two of my favorite subjects: about glass and about modern technology as we manufacture this product.*]

In actual fact, it was not a pleasure. This was my third presentation to a customer in recent weeks and here I was as Manager of Quality Assurance for my company standing in front of the executive management group of Coca Cola at their headquarters in Atlanta, Georgia. No other Owens Illinois executive wanted to do it; I inherited the job because I was the bottom of the totem pole.

> [*"Blending the two subjects together is fascinating because in talking one we address the modern space age, and in glass we find ourselves with one of the oldest commercial products of the world.*]

The tall guy in the front row wearing the turban was the Coca Cola Corporate Technical Director. I was familiar with his Egyptian background since he was featured in a recent article in Time Magazine that described Coke's international management. Reading between the lines, I detected the writer had discretely labelled him a cutthroat, which was consistent with the profile of some other Coke executives I had encountered.

[*"Glass is unique in many ways. The glass container is our most ancient package; yet, as you contemplate this past, visit your local supermarket and you will be pleasantly surprised at the many new, attractive, and innovative glass packages. While some glass containers are prized as antiques, others are sought after by the modish crowd as symbols of young people on the go.*]

I knew these beginning lines of my speech from memory and had often used them as a lead-in to the meat of a talk that would vary depending on who the audience was and my reason for being there. For this Coca Cola presentation the occasion was loaded with peril, which was why I was handed the thankless assignment. We knew this was a marriage between us and them that Coca Cola wanted to find a way out of – a divorce - but on their timing and terms. Their business was to sell liquid - the Coke product- and it rubbed them that they were dependent on my company, Owens Illinois, to furnish the glass containers to carry their product to market. They were embarrassed to focus on my company's product, the Coke glass bottle in their ads. The Coke long range strategy was to change that scenario and unshackle their company's dependence on the O-I product.

SLIDE #1: OBSIDIAN INDIAN ARROWHEAD

[*"A few years ago when backpacking in Yosemite, I found a black obsidian arrowhead. Obsidian is a natural glass formed from the lava of certain volcanoes. The Mono Indians of the early nineteenth century made obsidian utensils from the lava beds in Utah and Nevada and used them for trade as they travelled over the top of the Sierra Mountains.*]

The Coke conference auditorium was an impressive structure with a series of raised tiers that focused on the speaker's platform with a large movie screen immediately behind. I would be using that in my presentation with a cassette of slides showing our technology.

SLIDE #2: NASA MOON ROCK

[*"Our astronauts have determined the existence of glass particles on the moon — a natural phenomenon.*]

I had pondered how to make a presentation that did credit to my company without calling attention to the fact that Coke was dependent on us to carry their product to market; and decided to skirt the issue by focusing on the attributes of glass, its unique history, its marketing advantage, and our automated production processes that delivered a high quality product. I knew from feedback of prior speeches that the history of glass was always of interest. I started with this as a lead-in. The meat would come later.

[*"Pliny, the Roman Historian, tells his story of how the Phoenicians discovered glass many thousands of years ago. The Phoenicians were great seafaring merchants. One day, the crew of a trading vessel carrying a load of natron, soda ash, landed on a sandy beach along the Mediterranean Sea. The fire burned hot, fanned by the sea breeze. The next morning the sailors found a substance that glittered like ice in the sand. Later they realized that the hot fire had melted the beach sand and soda ash to form glass. From that time on, the Phoenicians knew the secret of glass making.*

No one knows if this story is true. It is likely though, because the first glass was made quite accidentally and in this part of the ancient world.]

My speech had started well. Most in the audience settled comfortably in rapt attention; however, the Egyptian Technical director postured like a bird of prey ready to pounce if anything was said that did not meet his liking.

> [*"The world's first glass containers were made in Egypt about 2000 BC. They were used for cosmetics, perfumes, and ointments. Because of the durability of glass, these containers, sometimes buried in the ground or in tombs for thousands of years, can be seen in museums today. We have several from ancient Egypt in our museum in Toledo.*]

SLIDE #3: PICTURE OF TOLEDO MUSEUM

The reference to Egypt sounded almost like it had been planned in regard to the Technical Director, but I had no idea it would fit so well. I kept my eyes away from the Egyptian, but wondered if he liked what he heard?

["*The earliest glass containers were made in various kinds of sand molds or by progressive dipping. A major step forward occurred about 300 BC when the blow tube was invented.*]

SLIDE #4: USING A BLOW TUBE

I took this photo in one of our O-I plants in Vineland, New Jersey, where the blow tube is still utilized to produce the large chemical carboys that could not be made any other way. Their Blow-Tube chamber looked like something out of a Boris Karloff movie where huge guys (with big lungs) blew into long pipes with a red-hot gob of glass on the end that slowly took the shape of a bottle. These husky guys swung the six-foot blow tubes back and forth with barely a grunt while the parison dangled on the end.

[*"The blow tube enabled craftsmen to make new kinds of containers, and particularly important was the ability to make them waterproof and air tight. Merchants began to ship oils, wine, honey, and other products on long sea voyages to other parts of the world.*

When Roman Emperors conquered Egypt, they demanded a tribute of glass. Then they ordered Egyptian craftsmen to come to Rome and train glass makers in their art. Archaeologists have recovered many glass objects from the Roman Empire.]

Opps! It was too late to pull that from the presentation and I knew evidence for this was skimpy but hoped the Egyptian Technical Director would take the reference to Egyptian craftsmen as a compliment.

[*"In the 14th century, an Island near Venice, Murano, became the center of the glassmaking craft with a lucrative export trade. The art of glassmaking was a closely held secret in this isolated environment, but the knowledge of how to make glass gradually spread to France and England.*

Glassmaking operations were usually located in a heavily forested area to provide wood for the hot fires needed. One such location was in the du Maurier region of the Lorie Valley in France; and a glassmaking descent, the famous author Daphne du Maurier, relates the family history during the era when her ancestors were caught up in the French Revolution of the early nineteenth century. Glasshouses during this era were crude structures enclosing a single furnace located in the midst of a forest that supplied wood for the fires, and the working crew and their families lived in this isolated environment.]

This book is a favorite of mine, perhaps because of the connection to glass, but I have found it is one of the few accounts that captures the passion and violence of the French Revolution. [1] *It is the story of a family of master glass craftsmen, and recreates the turbulent period from Louis XV to the ascendancy of Napoleon, when a man might wield supreme power one day and fall under the guillotine the next. Daphne du Maurier's ancestors were caught-up in the turmoil as marauding gangs from Paris came pilfering into their Lorie Valley area.*

---

[1] Daphne du Maurier, *The Glass Blower*, Doubleday & Company, Inc., 1963

SLIDE #5: A SAILING SHIP OF THAT EARLY ERA

["*In America, glass container manufacturing came along from the start. The year after Jamestown was settled, 1607, a ship sailed into the harbor with new supplies and some skilled craftsmen.*

Eight of these craftsmen were glass makers. These glass makers in the autumn of 1608 built the first factory in America and the product was glass. They used local materials: sand from the James River, potash from the forest, oyster shells for lime, and wood from the forest to provide the fires. This glass factory in the forest was little more than a hut with a main furnace and two small ones. All the furnaces were built with rough boulders. They produced glass products exported to England. This glasshouse was the first manufacturing factory in America.]

SLIDE #6: JUMBLE OF ROCKS IN JAMESTOWN

[*"What articles were produced is not known but from fragments of green glass found in the ruins of Jamestown it is thought they were vials, bottles, and drinking glasses.*]

I must have felt bold when preparing this draft because the historical evidence for this glass factory was meager. The original settlement of Jamestown had been overrun by local Indians and any glass factory, if it actually existed, was completely destroyed leaving nothing but scraps of debris for historians to ponder. I doubt these Coke executives had ever heard anything about the history of glass; so, I was free to say whatever historically fit my purpose and my purpose was to highlight the long tradition of glass.

[*"Incidentally, rather than using our Owens Illinois art specialists, I opted to do much the photography myself since it is a new hobby. This picture is the work from my basement so if you are critical of the artistry you can let me know later.*]

That brought a slight smile replacing the previous frown on the face of the Egyptian. Perhaps he would now settle back and enjoy my presentation – a commoner making his presentation to royalty.

In an O-I meeting where we discussed the reason for the invite from Coca Cola for a speaker from O-I to deliver an address to their corporate executive group, we were somewhat puzzled why the invitation, which was unusual in coming from Coke. Even more puzzling to me was why I was chosen for the job inasmuch as I had previous controversial encounters with their quality group in Atlanta. I had been put out on point by O-I management as a barrier to defend against their constant demand for a tightening of specifications, which would raise our production costs. We felt their motivation was not quality but rather a means to negotiate a lower price. I had been in their Atlanta headquarters only two months previously to discuss the specifications for the thickness of the sidewall of glass containers. Their manager of Quality had come on strong but after a lot of wrangling, I simply said "no", we did not agree with the tighter specs.

At the core of the conflict was our single service plasti-shield non-returnable container that was covered by polyethylene foam. My company had developed the design, which was standardized for the entire beverage industry, and its debut had been openly opposed by Coke. They had eventually come around to its use only after being forced with its success in the marketplace by their archrival, Pepsi. An industry-wide standardized beverage container was contrary to the strategy of Coca Cola. They wanted a unique product. Now our new plasti-shield container design had gone world-wide. A few months previously I had been in Kuala Lumpur, Malaysia, to provide assistance to our licensee who had one production line manufacturing the Plasti-shield container and a second production line producing the unique Coca Cola Mae West bottle shape. That historic returnable bottle shape was still utilized all over the world even though it had almost disappeared in the United States. The Owens Illinois and Coca Cola container strategies were at loggerheads with each other, and here I was standing in front of the adversary.

SLIDE #7: PHOTO OF PLASTI-SHIELD CONTAINER

[*"While art and beauty were important to many containers, in some cases they also serve a very functional purpose.*]

That is a direct statement in support of our plasti-shield container, and who could argue with that statement other than Coke who found it contrary to their marketing interests. I moved on fast to avoid any negative reaction to my rhetorical question.

[*"In France in the early part of the 19th century, Nicholas Appert had discovered how to preserve food by cooking it in air- tight glass jars, earning a prize from Napoleon who wanted the method to feed his army. This was the start of the canning industry."*]

SLIDE #8: PICTURE OF 19TH CENTURY LABORATORY

["In 1806, Sir Humphrey Davies discovered an artificial means for introducing carbonic acid into water creating the basis for the carbonated mineral water and the soft drink industry.

Some books credit Durand, a Philadelphia druggist as being the first to bottle mineral water in 1825.]

Now I would begin preaching to the choir as I focused on the beginnings of the Coca Cola product. I had done my research carefully to be sure and not leave any stone unturned or misplaced.

SLIDE #9: PICTURE OF EARLY-DAY DRUGSTORE

["*In 1825, in Atlanta, Georgia, an obscure druggist named Dr. John S. Pemberton, while working on a modification of a proprietary medicine called French Wine Coca, invented a new Drink, Coca Cola. The drink was offered for sale at a local soda fountain as a headache cure, and the rest is history.*]

I had researched this information about the beginnings of their product extensively and was able to supply references if challenged.

SLIDE #10: FIRST COCA COLA BOTTLE

["*The first coke bottle was embossed Joseph A. Biedenharn, the name of the first man to bottle the product in 1894 in Vicksburg, Mississippi.*

The first plant to bottle Coca Cola exclusively was opened in Chattanooga in 1899. These early bottles had Hutchinsen type of closure and finish, and they normally had the name of the bottler rather than Coca Cola embossed on the bottle."]

One of my hobbies was to collect bottles and I had an original Coca Cola bottle; however, it was not of particular value because there was nothing on the bottle to identify it as one of their original containers.

SLIDE #11: PHOTO OF COKE MAE WEST BOTTLE

[*"In 1915, the unique Hobble Skirt or Mae West shape was uniformly adopted for Coca Cola and it has remained relatively unchanged through the years, and is well recognized worldwide.*]

Now I had reached the meat of my presentation as I referred to the plasti-shield bottle.

SLIDE #12: PLASTI-SHIELD BOTTLE

["*In the 1970s and 80s, the Coca Cola name also went to market in the very attractive and functional 16 ounce single service plasti- shield package shown here.*"]

To avoid any negativism, I moved on quickly.

SLIDE #13: MANUAL PRODUCTIVITY

[*"At the end of the 19th century, glass bottle and jars were still being made exactly as they had been for 2000 years although the demand for glass containers had increased tremendously. The most that one glass blower and 4 assistants could make was about 18 dozen a day.*]

SLIDE #14: "OWENS" ROTATING FORMING MACHINE

["*In 1903, the first fully automatic bottle making machine was invented by Michael Owens. The Owens name comes down to us today in the name Owens- Illinois. Our present day O-I formed in the year 1929 through the merger of the Owens Bottle Machine Company and the Illinois Glass Company. Our predecessor companies go back to the 19th century New England Glass Company.*]

SLIDE #15: OWENS HOLDING A HOT PARISON

[*"The invention of the automatic machine did much more for glass than merely increase its output. Of great importance was the opportunity it presented for standardization of design and then as a further outgrowth the development of quality assurance procedures. Once a product is produced under standard, reproducible, and controllable conditions that product becomes far more functional.*

I have traced this brief thumbnail sketch of the history of the glass container because I find there is a fascination in the product that is so very ancient and at the same time so very modish and avant-garde in the market places of the world.

Let me now turn to the subject of how glass is made and the physical and chemical properties. One reason that glass has always been universally accepted and used is found in the basic raw materials from which it is made, and the unique properties of glass.]

Most of the coke executives in the audience do not have a clue on how a bottle is manufactured, which is one reason they ask for ever tighter specifications. I have escorted dozens of customers as visitors through our factories, but never once in all the years did I ever see a coke visitor. I don't know if they had a policy against it, or just a lack of interest; nevertheless, I intended to present a picture of complexity in glass manufacturing so they would become more understanding of the issues involved in tightening the specifications of a glass container.

SLIDE #16: PHOTO OF THE O-I IONE SAND PLANT

[*"Glass is made from Silica (ordinary sand), limestone, and soda-ash in roughly in the same proportions as they occur in the crust of the earth. So these plentiful and inexpensive raw materials have formed an economic base for glass that has seen it through the centuries and in all parts of the world, and that remains a fundamental strength of glass today. Cullet and recycled glass is also an important component for making glass.*]

I had to suppress the urge to call attention to our great recycling program for glass containers or include a mention that our potential packing competitor, the plastic bottle, was not recyclable. I knew Coke was considering moving part of their packaging to the plastic bottle. In addition to being the largest producer of glass in the United States and world-wide, Owens Illinois was also the largest producer of plastic bottles; so, I was prevented from bad-mouthing plastic bottles, one of my company's own products.

SLIDE #17: BATCH HOUSE

["*Now that we see what glass is made from, let's see how we mass produce glass containers. We start at the batch house where we store and mix the raw materials. From storage bins, precise quantities are mixed and delivered to the glass furnace.*"]

SLIDE #18: DELIVERING BATCH TO FURNACE

["*Batch is delivered from the batch house to the furnaces in older factories by batch bucket carriers and in newer factories by conveyors under computer control directly from the batch house to the furnaces.*"]

SLIDE #19: PICTURE INSIDE FURNACE

["*This is a photo taken through a 6 inch port looking inside a furnace that is under operation. The natural gas is fired as it heats the molten glass up to 2500° degrees Fahrenheit. The raw material is fed into the front end of the furnace by screws, and gradually melts as it passes from the front to the back end of the furnace, which will take two or three hours. These glass furnaces full of molten glass are typically twenty feet across, thirty feet from front to back, and six feet deep. They are comparable to a swimming pool full of molten glass. As a result of this harsh environment and the erosion by the raw material, a furnace must be idled every six or seven years and refractory sidewalls replaced. As you would anticipate the costs of furnace operation and repair are quite large, and the operation of a glass furnace requires considerable expertise.*]

SLIDE #20: SCHEMATIC DIAGRAM OF FURNACE

["*This diagram shows a top view of a typical furnace layout. The molten glass travels through a two foot square orifice from the melting furnace into the forehearth, a small furnace, where it is further mixed and the temperature is stabilized. Then the molten glass flows into feeders, which are troughs that carry the glass out over the forming machine.*]

SLIDE #21: PHOTO OF FEEDER

["*The feeder is the first step for the glass molten state in its journey into the solid state that we will recognize as a glass container. At this point in its travels it is red hot at 2300° degrees Fahrenheit. The molten glass drops down from the feeder in a stream that is sheared into individual chunks of glass that are called gobs.*]

SLIDE #22: SHEARING STREAM INTO GOBS

["These gobs fall into chutes where they are guided to drop into to one of the individual sections of the IS (Individual Section) forming machine. The gob then begins a two part process to achieve the shape of the finished container.]

SLIDE #23: GOB TRAVELING DOWN THE CHUTE

["*The gob then begins the forming process in the IS forming machine. It first enters the blank mould in an upside-down position and the mould closes around it. It is here where the finish is formed, a small cavity created, and the molten parison is formed into a rough preliminary shape of the ultimate finished container.*]

SLIDE #24: PARISON TRANSFERRED TO FINAL MOULD

["*The parison is then inverted and transferred to the final mould. This forming process takes less time than it takes to describe it, normally spending less than two seconds total in the IS forming machine manufacturing processes.*"]

SLIDE #25: PARISON BLOWN INTO FINAL SHAPE

["*In the final mould, the parison is blown into the shape of the mould.*]

SLIDE #26: BOTTLE LIFTED BY TAKE-OUT TONGS

["*Take-out tongs lift the finished bottle shape from the IS forming machine final mould and sets it down on the conveyor belt for transit into the annealing lehr. It now has the shape of the container. As the bottle leaves the IS forming machine it has cooled to 900° Fahrenheit; hence, considerable heat has been removed by cooling fans as it was processed during those few seconds though the forming process. How this enormous heat removal process is performed is one of the challenges of the bottle-making process that separates the expert from the novice.*]

SLIDE #27: PICTURE OF IS FORMING MACHINE

["*The IS (Individual Section) forming machine has replaced the former rotary Owens Machine in the modern factory. It is the world-wide state-of-the-art means of producing glass containers. There have been many improvements to this basic machine to obtain a more assured level of higher quality together with increased productivity. Earlier designs of 4 section single gob forming machines were speed limited to about 50 bottles per minute, and these speeds were improved dramatically was we installed 6 section and 8 section IS machines; and we now have 10 section 4 gob (quads} IS machines that can product glass containers at speeds upward of 2000 B.P.M., and with an even higher level of quality.*]

SLIDE #28: BOTTLE IN TRANSIT TO LEHR ENTRANCE

["*Glass temperatures have now gone from approximately 2300 ° at the feeder, to 1200° in the forming machine to around 900° as the bottle enters the lehr. Here it is semi- molten.*

Bottles are fed into the lehr to be reheated to 1000 ° F. and then slowly cooled during transit over an hour's time to relieved any residual stress and complete the forming process. The making of a glass container involves the controlled removal of heat from 2300 ° to room temperature as it exits the lehr.]

SLIDE #29: SPRAY SURFACE TREATMENT

[*"As bottles near the end of the lehr, they receive a surface treatment that protects and lubricates their surfaces and preserves their inherent strength.*]

SLIDE #30: TRANSFER FROM LEHR TO CONVEYORS

[*"Bottles transfer from the lehr onto conveyors. This is a complex mixing operation in which bottles leave the seven-foot wide web lehr belt and are herded onto a single-line four-inch wide conveyor. When bottles are manufactured on a four- section IS machine single gob at the rate of about 50 bottles per minute, this re- alignment operation is relatively simple; however, when they are manufactured on a ten-section quad IS machine at a rate of 2000 bottles per minute, as will be discussed later, it becomes a higher level of complexity.*]

SLIDE #31: PLUG GAUGE

[*"Every bottle has a plug inserted through the finish to insure a free passage for a customer's fill tube, and the same plug checks that the outside diameter is correct for the closure that will be used.*]

SLIDE #32: FP-5 AUTOMATIC INSPECTION MACHINE

[*"This is a photo of an FP-5 machine, one of the first automatic gauging and inspection devices that every bottle will be subjected to. In this unit, the bottles are rotated. A multitude of tasks within the FP machine for a rotating bottle are undertaken in this device, depending on the type of container and its end use. An example of the tasks completed for a single service plasti-shield container is the following sequence of operations: optical inspection of the finish area with the use of a refractory-detection device; optical inspection of the sidewall, optical inspection of the bottom and heel of the rotating bottle; mechanical gauging of the diameter of the finish; and mechanical gauging of the diameter and out-of-round of the sidewall. An RF (radio frequency) gauge measures the thickness the sidewall of the rotating bottle to determine thickness. An optical device will also read the cavity number on the bottom of the bottle that is marked with a digital readout, and the cold end selector can indicate cavities for rejection.*]

This simple description does not do adequate justice to the multitude of automatic inspection devices utilized in the cold end to detect and discard defects and flaws in the glass containers as they moved along chain conveyors belts. Early in my career as an engineer I was actively involved in their initial development and later after I had become a manager I became a leader in pursuing their utilization in factories.

The most valuable cold end development was the Cavity Identification Device. Concentric rings on the bottoms of bottles were coded with binary information that could be combined with defect information and isolate a production problem, which was a big asset on a ten quad machine that had 40 different mold cavities. Cavity identification became the hub of computerization.

The development that revolutionized the forming process was the digital IS machine. The rotating timing drum that had controlled the sequence of operations in the forming machine with this analog device for a century was replaced with a small box full of electronics that accomplished that task under digital control. This network coordination extended above the machine to the feeder where shears cut the hot glass stream into individual gobs at a rate of hundreds per minute, chutes delivered these gobs to one of ten individual sections each with 4-cavity mold, the sequence of actions of each section of the machine that varied depending on its off-set from the centerline were controlled, take-out tongs lifted the bottles from the machine at hundreds per minute and set them on conveyors without touching each other, and push-in arms at the entrance of the lehr moved rows of bottles into the lehr to begin their transit from the hot end to room temperature in the cold end. All these movements interfaced with each other, and lacking good coordination the result was turmoil.

The digital controlled IS machine of O-I had no competitor anywhere in the world, and was quickly adopted by oversea affiliates and licensees. It gave O-I technical superiority of productivity and quality throughout of worldwide glass industry.

These technical developments became essentially the core of the O-I business as it expanded to overseas opportunities. There were virtually no competitors with comparable mechanization that led to such high quality and increasing productivity. As a result of this technical capability, O-I gradually became dominant world-wide.

SLIDE #33: FORMING MACHINE OPERATOR

[*"This is a forming machine operator who is monitoring the operation of an IS forming machine. His job is to insure lubrication and keep the machine operating properly.*]

This photo does not do justice to the harsh environment of the forming department. The IS machines operate with compressed air and cooling wind from fans and compressors. The combined noise level of the cooling wind and the steady pulsing of compressed air that moves the machine components through their cycle produce a noise level in which conversation is difficult. A foreman must talk directly into the ear of a machine operator to be heard. Ear plugs and safety glasses are mandatory.

SLIDE #34: INSPECTING AND PACKING BOTTLES

[*"A selector is inspecting bottles during the process of packing them into a carton.*]

The workforce of a glass factory is unique because of the nature of the unusual environment that is created by the huge glass furnaces that operates continuously at elevated temperatures, the cooling wind and compressed air of the IS machines, and the noise level of hundreds of conveyors that operate in the hot end and cold end for transporting the bottles. Wearing ear plugs and safety glasses is mandatory for the workforce of the entire factory.

The twenty-four hours of operation seven days each week requires skilled workers on four continuously rotating shifts. Male and female workers as well as also their families must adjust to ever changing day and night rotating schedules in their personal lives in the factory and also at home and in the community. That unusual environment of rotating shift work has existed in a glass house since ancient times. Daphne du Maurier describes the same scenario with her ancestors in France three hundred years ago. She has observed: *"The laws, customs, and privileges of the glass makers were strictly observed. … There's was a closed community."* [2]

---

[2] Daphne du Maurier, *The Glass Blower*, Double Day & Co. 1963, p. 14

SLIDE #35: SUPERVISORY CONTROL COMPUTER

["*The output from every inspection device is fed into a computer located at each operating shop in the cold end and this information is available to personnel who monitor the quality of the product. It is also fed to hot end and is available to the forming machine operator. As a result of the timely information generated, personnel are able to provide stronger monitoring and control functions of the finished product.*]

The Forming Supervisory Control Computer and also the Selecting Supervising Control Computer from each production shop in the factory can also be monitored by operating managers throughout the factory and also by Technical Center specialists in Toledo where they can interface with the factory automation.

SLIDE #36: AUTOMATIC PACKING

[*"This is a photo of an automated packing operation. Prior to being packed, each bottle is inspected by a skilled selector who inspects each bottle as it is rotated and passes in front of a light-plate mounted alongside the conveyor belt.*]

When I became the Finish Product Manager at the Oakland Plant, there were 26 IS forming machines in operation, each producing a different container. These were contained in a factory that filled a city block. The plant had a workforce of a two thousand employees. I was Finish Product Manager in charge of all departments in the cold end that included everything after the annealing lehrs. These six departments numbered about a thousand employees and included eight hundred personnel who selected, inspected and packed the containers into corrugated boxes and palletized the loads for shipment.

The 1960's when I became a manager in the Oakland Plant were revolutionary times of social change. It was at the height of the Vietnam War protests and there were antiwar riots on East 14th Street two blocks from the Oakland Plant. The grape picker conflict in the vineyards was active. The social movements involving equal rights for blacks and for females were active and we had large populations of all of these working in the plant. When I arrived on the job as a manager there were no females above the entry level jobs anywhere in the factory. During the five years of my leadership during the 1960's that was to change dramatically; for example, the first females promoted to the position of a salaried shift foreman occurred under my watch. It was a time of social revolution throughout the nation, and also within my factory.

SLIDE #37: BULK-PACK OF BOTTLES

[*"Most of the containers are packed into cardboard packages, but many are also placed in bulk-pack loads in which tier sheets separate layers of bottle-to-bottle containers and this 7-foot high load is encased in a tight plastic wrap.*]

Inasmuch as the factory also had a complete corrugated operation starting with roll-stock from paper mills that produced corrugated cartons and inter-packing, the company preferred to keep customers utilizing cartons, which were a high profit item; however, the bulk pack option was gradually becoming the favorite choice of customers because it represented efficiencies for them. The factory had to develop the technology of how to bulk pack and prepare these unstable loads for storage and shipment. We accommodated to the customers wishes and gradually became a leader in bulk pack operations.

SLIDE #38: AUTOMATIC CARTON PALLETIZING

["*This is a photo of an automatic palletizing operation in which dozens of cartons are assembled into a stable pallet load for a truckload shipment to the customer.*]

SLIDE #39: WAREHOUSE AISLE WITH PALLETS

["*In one of our many warehouses, the pallets of containers are stored awaiting shipment to our customer's processing facility. Huge warehouses allow us to store product that is available to meet the scheduling needs that may develop within the customer's operation.*"]

We had acres of warehouse full of pallet-loads stored four pallets high in long aisles. In the Oakland plant we had five in-plant warehouses on-site plus several more rented elsewhere.

SLIDE #40: ALUMINUM CAN AND PLASTIC BOTTLE

["*We recognize that a customer will have other choices for packaging their product. We also have experience with some of these, for example, in a Perrysburg facility we pack aluminum cans under contract for some customers and the O-I Plastic Bottle division of O-I is also the world's largest producer of plastic bottles. These operations give us valuable packaging experience.*]

SLIDE #41: MECHANICAN PROPERTIES

[*"The properties of glass have generally been known and appreciated for generations. Among the mechanical properties is the unique combination that when hot it is vicious and can be formed into many different shapes, and as it cools it is hard and durable.*

Pristine glass has extremely high tensile strength, of the same order of magnitude as steel, about 50,000 psi. Since it can lose much strength when subjected to abrasion, its actual strength is determined by the condition of its surface. We utilize two methods to deal with this: a lubricious surface coating and the second means is to protect critical surfaces with polyethylene form as is done with the familiar plasti- shield bottle.]

Another mention of the plasti-shield bottle, which has provided O-I with the advantage of standardization in the marketplace, but at the same time, it caused Coca Cola to lose their unique container image. I should move-on fast to avoid highlighting this.

SLIDE #42: CHEMICAL PROPERTIES

[*"Among the chemical properties of glass, the most notable is its excellent chemical durability. Glass is virtually inert from a chemical standpoint. It puts nothing into the product and takes nothing from it. Glass is impermeable, non-porous, sanitary and odorless. Firmly sealed bottles are air- thigh and moisture proof.*]

SLIDE #43: OPTICAL PROPERTIES

["*With respect to the optical properties of glass, the most obvious is transparency. Also is the ability to vary color and visual impact with the additions of ingredients such carbon tri-valent chrome to create a multitude of colors: flint, ambers, Georgia green, emerald green and others.*

The amount of visual light in the 400- 700 millimeter range transmitted by glass is a function of its thickness, color, and certain light-absorbing ingredients. This is also true for ultra-violet light in the 300-400 millimeter range. Amber passes less than half the ultra-violet light as flint, and green even less.

At a time some twenty years ago, O-I began to make a green glass at the request of some wine and soft drink customers with the addition of the special ingredient hexa-valent chrome, which absorbed more ultra-violet. We called this glass Ultra-sorb. We then conducted some internal chemical and taste tests and concluded that this special glass was an unnecessary expense for soft drinks with no discernable benefit to flavor under normal conditions of use. Later it was also identified as a possible carcinogenic. For this reason we immediately stopped its manufacture and we alerted all our world-wide affiliates and associates to do the same.]

I anticipated some follow-up questions on this explosive issue of carcinogenic hexa-valent chrome, and to insure to be fully prepared, spent a morning with the chemists in our O-I Technical Center and with company lawyers to educated myself and prepare responses. To my surprise, I learned that the only glassmaker in the world still producing this carcinogenic glass to our knowledge was an O-I affiliate in Japan, and they were doing it to meet the specific requirements for Coca Cola Japan. I did not intend to comment further on the issue, but I was prepared to respond if the Egyptian Technical Director thought he had a "got-you" and wanted to pursue the issue further in hopes he could "put some egg on our face." What's good for the goose is good for the gander; I'm ready – let him bring it on!

SLIDE #44: MORE ON PHYSICAL PROPERTIES

["*I want to return to physical properties and mention a couple more attributes of glass. One is the tensile strength of glass that allows it to contain internal hydrostatic pressure. This property is of course why glass has been the container of choice for carbonated soft drinks from the time of their conception over a hundred years ago. Most of our soft drink glass containers are designed to withstand up to 5 gas volumes. We make champagne containers to withstand even higher pressures. This attribute of glass that allows the flavor benefits of carbonation to be retained over a long period of time is unique when it is found in combination with all the other chemical and physical properties.*

A second physical property worth a mention is the rigidity of glass which is of great benefit in the design of closure systems, and particularly where internal pressure is involved. It is difficult to design leak-proof closure systems unless one of the meeting surfaces will provide a rigid backstop for the other flexible surfaces to press against. No other package material in use will match the glass finish in this regard.]

SLIDE #45: COMPUTERS

[*"Let me now turn to the use of computers within O-I and trace their utilization through three phases in the history of their development.*]

SLIDE #46: ANALOG COMPUTERS

[*"The first phase developed many years ago, almost from ancient times, and grew rapidly during World War Two. In the late 40's and early 50's when I was a naval officer during the Korean War, the analog computer was the state–of-art. These computers operate with measurable quantities and use wheels, gears, levers, mirrors and electrical impulses to accomplish their computer magic.*]

As a midshipman on a summer training cruise, I helped operate the Mod-One fire-control computer aboard the battleship, USS Iowa. It was the largest analog computer ever made, measuring 5 ft. square and 5 ft. tall; and it controlled aiming of the gun turrets fore and aft when the battleship was underway in rolling seas. My role was to look interested and stay out-of-the-way while naval specialist managed the computer inputs.

SLIDE #47: IS FORMING MACHINE TIMING DRUM

["*The timing drum of an IS machine was an analog computer that exercised direct control of each individual section of the forming machine. As the timing drum rotates, it controlled the movements of each individual section of the bottle machine as it moved through its cycle. The rotating drum pushes raised nobs to actuate valves that control compressed air that determines what mechanical movements will take place in a sequence one-after-the-other.*]

SLIDE #48: DIGITAL COMPUTER

["*A second watershed phase for computers occurred in the early 1950's when I was in graduate school in Berkeley. This was the development of the digital computer. O-I had already begun to use these in office systems when I joined in 1954. They were a giant step forward for the office, but early models were a disappointment on the factory floor where they were unable to adapt to the heat and harsh environment. We used them, but with difficulty. They were costly, troublesome to operate, and had serious reliability problems. For example, we had to locate our consoles in air conditioned rooms because of the great amount of heat generated, and we had to be ready to spring into action with backup analog or manual systems whenever a computer broke down, which was often.*]

SLIDE #49: THE MICROCHIP

["*In the middle of the 1970's, we witnessed a watershed phase in the glasshouse with the invention of the microchip. Suddenly we had small and powerful computers that were low cost and could operate with high reliability in the harsh environment of the factory.*

When the microchip was developed, we were ready to capitalize on it, and we have taken leaps ahead with this new technology. We installed microchip computer inputs throughout the hot and cold end of the factory to improve the monitoring and control of production.

We have also made effective use of other modern technology such as lasers, robots, computer-aided machinery, micro- processors, mini-computers, and other space age hardware. Let me tell you some ways we utilize these.]

SLIDE #50: BATCH HOUSE

["*The batch house is where we bring in and mix our raw materials. This was one of the first operations we computerized over a decade ago. We had been plagued with problems of placing material in wrong storage bins, and problems with the control of batch mixing. We solved those problems with computerization and also eliminated virtually all the manpower at the same time. It was a win-win.*]

SLIDE #51: FURNACE OPERATION

["Our furnace operation is now controlled by a computer which monitors fuel input, temperatures at various locations, pressures, exhaust gases, and molten glass level. Perhaps the biggest story here is not the computer so much as the thermo- processors which are able to measure temperatures in this harsh environment up to the 3000° F temperature level, and accomplish it with accuracy and reliability. This is the same temperature range that space age astronauts deal with during re- entry.]

SLIDE #52: IS FORMING MACHINE

["*Our IS forming machine, which was formerly controlled by the timing drum is now under the control of a digital computer. Gone are the rotating drums that were marginally inaccurate and a danger for the operator to adjust. Each individual section of the machine is independently monitored and controlled under digital computer control.*

These mini-computers for each individual section of the forming machine are linked to a second computer that we call the Forming Supervisory Control Computer. This gives us a tool by which we can troubleshoot or evaluate machine performance. Incidentally, this can be accomplished either at the plant by plant personnel or over a phone link interfaced with our Technical Center in Toledo where specialists can assist in the analysis.]

SLIDE #53: LASERS

[*"One of our O-I products is the glass for use in lasers, and we also employ these instruments in our operations, particularly as control devices in our furnace operations.*]

SLIDE #54: ROBOTICS

["We make extensive use of robotics, although there is some possible debate over what qualifies as a robot. We don't have any R2D2's running around. I'd define a robot as a machine with self-contained intelligence that performs mechanical functions, and we do make extensive use of robot systems in various inspective and handling activities.]

SLIDE #55: CAVITY IDENTIFICATION

["*One of the important developments we accomplished in the 70's we call CID, which is Cavity Identification Device. We place rings or other such markings on the bottoms or heels of our bottle designs, and these are coded with binary information. These markings enable us to automatically identify the specific machine section and mold cavity that produced each bottle.*

This CID capability has become a powerful new resource. Most of our quality efforts must address the individual cavity. Now that this can be done automatically and coupled with the automatic inspection devices, it has opened up the entire quality control function to direct computer control.]

SLIDE #56: AUTOMATIC PRESSURE TESTING

[*"Let me describe a system that performs automatic pressure testing. On a quad 10 IS forming machine we product bottles simultaneously from 40 different mold cavities and the internal pressure characteristics will vary and be unique to each cavity. Our computer that has an internal time clock will call for a sample from each of these 40 sections. These will be conveyed into a robotic system where it is filled with water and subjected to internal pressure until the failure level is reached. The computer records and analyzes the results, reaches a decision, and calls for a retest if necessary. The computer has been programmed to use the switching rule concepts of the Military Standards tables, which reduces the frequency of tests for good cavities and increases the frequency for marginal cavities. With this fully robotic system, we improve our quality control capability while also eliminating a substantial labor cost. We have one of these units operational in our nearby Atlanta plant.*]

SLIDE #57: COMPUTER REVIEW

[*"Let me conclude my computer review with the observation that we use this modern technology very pragmatically and not because it is a modish thing to do. Each system stands on the merits of its own performance, each must be economically justified and indeed, we continue to be excited about advances we are making with this modern technology.*]

I was a manager in the Oakland and Los Angeles plants supplying on-site leadership during the two decades when these developments were first utilized on-line, and was quality Assurance Manager at the division level to continue in this role on a wider basis in all our domestic and world-wide factories.

SLIDE #58: COMPANY INTERNATIONAL ROLE

["*The technology I have been describing is in use in one or more of our domestic glass container plants but the company's arms reach well beyond the nation's borders. O-I has a proprietary or technical assistance relationship involving 266 manufacturing facilities in 24 countries. Collectively, they produce one-half the glass containers in the world. Their technology, of course, varies widely from place to place. In many of our international affiliates the state-of- art is close to our own and in some other places there is a decade leap backward in time. In many of our overseas affiliates, one of their customers is often Coca Cola; so, we share a worldwide impact with glass containers. I recently went to Kuala Lumpur, Malaysia, to assist with a problem and found a Coke plasti-shield bottle on one shop and the familiar Coke Mae West shape on the shop alongside. I expressed surprise they made both designs. They responded: they produce the returnable for their traditional market, but prefer the plasti-shield because it gives them a higher financial return and represents their future in the soft drink market of Asia.*

I can personally relate to the O-I overseas operations because one of my collateral duties as Manager of Quality Assurance for the 24 factories and sales branches of our domestic operations is the responsibility to also provide consulting assistance to the 266 plants of our international Division, and I have personally spent time in fifty of our overseas plants where I provided on-site management consulting assistance.]

SLIDE #59: THE 10 QUAD IS FORMING MACHINE

["*Our most advanced state-of-the-art production unit is the 10 quad. This IS forming machine has 10 individual sections with molds that produce 4 bottles each cycle. It can manufacture beer and soft drink bottles at much higher rates than ever seen before. The feeder controls, gob delivery system inputs, and the conveyor lines that carry the container outputs are computerized, and I question if we could successfully operate such machines and related hardware at the present high speeds without the use of computerization.*"]

SLIDE #60: QUALITY

["*Let's talk quality. It is a degree of excellence in a product, particularly that as seen through the eyes of the user. In that regard, in packaging we face double jeopardy. We must first meet the quality needs of the bottler for a container that can be successfully and efficiently processed and filled in their own operation. Then as the completed package goes to market, our package must also meet the quality and product integrity needs of the consumer in a competitive market environment.*

The degree of excellence in this package, its quality image, perhaps more than any other factor will determine which products are given shelf space. Market research has consistently shown the high quality image associated with glass containers.

What is the consumer interested in? That will vary from time to time and place to place, but certainly for your products, these consumer concerns will include such factors as image, price, aesthetics, quality, and product integrity.

Why Glass? Because it offers these things.

This ancient package uses modern technology to remain as a high quality – low cost package.

Glass is chemically virtually inert.

It is strong and tough; not only because of its special ingredients, but also because of the way it is made and cooled.

Glass can withstand temperature changes, resist pressure, and does not corrode.

Glass is impermeable, transparent, non- porous, sanitary and odorless.

Firmly sealed bottles and jars are air- tight and moisture proof.

Glass containers can be made in many unique, attractive and functional designs.

Above all, glass containers carry the image of a premium and quality package.

In the days of Augustus Caesar, and in fact, for nearly 3000 years, the glass bottle and jars were a luxury. Today, they are an everyday necessity.

Thank You.]

I walked from the podium and sat. The Coca Cola host took over and after thanking me, announced that I had agreed to answer any questions. The question and answer event was short-lived because of my answer to the first question. I saw the Egyptian Technical Director whisper to his assistant alongside, who then asked.

"*Is the hexavalent chrome that is a carcinogenic still being produced by O-I anywhere in the world?*

"*Yes,* I responded. "*It is produced by a licensee despite our strong recommendation to immediately stop producing it.*

I was ready with this response that I had rehearsed with our legal and International people.

"*O-I was alarmed when we learned it was a carcinogenic, so we immediately drained the furnace and dumped any production already made. At the same time we notified all our worldwide affiliates and associates of the jeopardy this material possessed and recommended they immediately follow suit and stop producing the glass. To our knowledge, the only one still producing the hexavalent chrome carcinogenic glass is an affiliate in Japan, and they continue to produce it to meet the express requirements of their customer, Coca Cola Japan. If you have any clout with this franchise, you may want to have a discussion with them on the subject.*

After my response, the Egyptian Technical Director made a hasty exit. There were a few other scattered questions and the event was finally concluded.

EPILOGUE

That speech to the Coca Cola executive management group was delivered in 1984, thirty five years ago. My reactions as I delivered the speech are as I remember them.

In the years since there have been some big changes in the industry, while at the same time the traditions of the glasshouse remain about the same as they were hundreds of years ago. It is a unique environment found almost nowhere else in any other industry; in my many oversea consulting assignments I witnessed it everywhere. At its core, the glasshouse is still essentially a family affair, and husband- wife teams and family ties predominate. When activity increases during the summer months there are usually offspring of employees working on summer jobs (including three of my own). In the Oakland plant where I was Finish Product Manager, we had several dozen instances where the husband was a hot-end Forming Machine Operator and his wife a cold-end Selector with the duty to discard any defective bottles she found. Glasshouse tradition was the glue that made it all work.

Perhaps the biggest changes within O-I occurred in recent decades as it became the behemoth that dominated the domestic and worldwide glass industry. Other glass container companies could not successfully compete with the high quality and productivity standards of O-I. Today, one half of the glass containers in the world are produced by the domestic and international factories owned by O-I; and most of the companies that had previously been associates and affiliates have now become owned by O-I.

I am somewhat ambivalent about my role as a consultant with the task of improving operations of the Kimble Division and Plastic Bottle Division and leading them to reach compliance and registration to the ISO 9000 Standard. After I completed this task, making them of greater value, these Divisions were then sold by O-I to other companies. Many of the managers and hourly workers in these Divisions had become personal friends, and the end result of our shared efforts was to cause them to be no longer an employee of O-I. Alas, such is the downside of progress.

Coca Cola is no longer a customer of any significance for the O-I domestic operations; and Coke has achieved their long-range strategy of taking their product to market in their own containers, either a plastic bottle they product in-house or an aluminum can; however, Coca Cola is still a major customer of O-I factories in oversea markets with returnable glass containers.

The ill-fated plasti-shield container is no more. The writing-on-the-wall became evident even before I retired because the process of applying the wrap was a troublesome burden in busy plants, and it never lived up to its projected economic benefits. I played a role in its demise.

I took a retirement package three years after this speech in 1987 at the age of 58 with 31 years of employment. The President of O-I asked me to continue working as a part-time consultant and assist the other divisions of the company with their quality programs and operating cultures. He attributed much of the quality culture in the Glass Container Division to the strong leadership I had provided to the factories and asked me to accomplish the same in other parts of the company. During the next few years I worked with the Kimble Division after their market share had taken a nosedive due to poor quality and competitors in Germany and Japan were eating their lunch. It took me three years to establish a new quality culture in their factories. I was no longer needed after their share of the market had returned to prior levels and they were again the worldwide industry leader. That experience was repeated with the Plastic Bottle division. After several years, the emphasis of my consulting turned to assisting O-I operations in reaching compliance with the ISO 9000 Standard (International Standards Organization). It was an excellent standard that emphasized the basics as they applied to a glass factory. Working with Terry Burns of Burns Associates, I assisted Kimble, the Plastic Bottle Division, and all the factories of the Glass Container Division in reaching compliance and registration with the ISO 9000 Standard. After reaching compliance with the Standard, which greatly increased their value in international markets, O-I sold both Kimble and the Plastic Product Division. Kimble was sold to a German company and the Plastic Products Division to a huge American conglomerate. Finally, the last components of O-I still needing to reach compliance with the ISO Standard were the headquarters departments in Toledo; and after this was accomplished my role as a consultant was concluded.

After working fifteen years as a part—time consultant (about two weeks per month) I finally retired after fifteen years in 2002 at 73 years of age. These were the best working years of my entire O-I employment. The day-to-day stresses that are a burden to an operational quality manager were no longer part of my job.

I was well qualitied for this consulting job; I had been well tested. After combat duty in Korea as a naval officer and a Master Degree in engineering, I had worked in four factories for 18 years prior to my move to O-I headquarters where I was appointed the Division Manager of Quality Assurance. I was familiar with all the highs and Lows of factory operations and knew many of the glasshouse problems because I had personally experienced them myself. Then in my Division role as Quality Manager, I provided leadership to the 24 domestic factories of O-I and also provided on-site assistance to 50 oversea factories of the International Division. I had a large and experienced staff. I knew glasshouse operations and I could spend a day in a glass factory anywhere in the world and have a sense of what was going good and where there were problems.

In my role as a consultant, I developed a special technique that I often utilized; some workers in most factories knew the "lay of the land", and my task was to identify these people, solicit their input, evaluate it against my own experience, and then react with my conclusions. In essence, my recommendations to the management of a factory were essentially based on input from some of their own workers together with my experience and conclusions. I was surprised at how many managers worldwide are tone deaf to communications from their own crews.

Oftentimes, my role as a consultant was as referee. Some companies had no way to measure if their quality was good or bad, which sometimes led to conflict between their factory and sales people or their own management. Under those circumstances, my stature as Quality Manager of the biggest and best glass operation in the world carried weight; I used great care to insure I did not abuse this asset.

I will close with a final observation: In the book that told of her family's culture in the glasshouse two-hundred years ago in France, Madame Daphne du Maurier highlights a truism that remains the same today all over the world:

"The glass world is unique. ... It had its own rules and customs. ... Instituted heaven knows how many centuries ago." [3]

I spent a 50 year lifetime career with O-I in the glass industry, and it was always fascinating to have a role at the mantle of this ancient product.

---

[3] Daphne du Maurier, *The Glass Blower*, Doubleday & Company, 1956, p.13

Printed in the United States
By Bookmasters